QUOTES
& NOTES

Hope you enjoy,
John Austin

QUOTES & NOTES

A Dad's Best Advice for His Kids

JOHN AUSTIN

Quotes & Notes: A Dad's Best Advice for His Kids

Copyright © 2022 by John Austin

All rights reserved. No part of this book may be reproduced, scanned, or distributed in any printed or electronic form without permission in writing from the publisher, except by a reviewer, who may quote brief passages in a review.

We have done our best to give proper credit to the original authors of the quotes in this book.

ISBN: 979-8-9860682-0-6 (Paperback)
ISBN: 979-8-9860682-1-3 (eBook)

Library of Congress Control Number: LCCN 2022906174

Cover design and interior formatting by
Becky's Graphic Design®, LLC
www.BeckysGraphicDesign.com

Printed in the U.S.A.

To my wife Michelle,
who deserves much more
credit than me for the smiles you may
notice on the pages of this book.

TABLE OF CONTENTS

Introduction ix
Character... 1
Abraham Lincoln's Road to the White House 14
Courage 23
A Confederate Soldier's Prayer 39
Faith 41
Family 51
Friendship..63
Happiness 73
Humorous 79
The Man in the Arena 88
Leadership 89
I've Learned 93
Life.. 97
Love 119
Love and Forgiveness... 125
Love and Kindness 129
Love and Marriage.. 135
Money 139
The Bixby Letter..143
Politics 147
The Spoken Word 153
Sports... 163
Success 169
Wisdom 179
Work...201
I Wish You Enough 215
Irish Blessing..216
Acknowledgments 217
About the Author..219

Alex, Mary, Michelle, and Aubrey, Avignon France 2016

Introduction

I became enamored with quotes in my teenage years. I was trying out for the high school basketball team, and read John Wooden's book "They Call Me Coach". At the beginning of each chapter, he included a quote, some of which you will see in this book. I discovered that quotes were short enough to be remembered, and memorable enough to recall when faced with a dilemma, a decision, or a difficult time in my life.

I was accepted to medical school after three years of college, trained to become a heart surgeon, and married my very lovely wife Michelle. We had three children, boy-girl twins Alex and Aubrey in 1992, and a daughter Mary Katherine in 1995. Around 2005, when the twins reached their teenage years, I wanted to give them good advice and encouragement, despite their occasional reluctance to accept it. I tumbled to the idea of writing quotes on a yellow sticky pad and putting them on the refrigerator before I left for work. I was practicing cardiac surgery at the time, and often would leave before they awoke, or miss dinners, or spend the night at the hospital, and I was acutely aware that my profession had a propensity for wayward children, or bad parenting, or both. And, in a moment of self-revelation, I discovered that like Michel de Montaigne, "I quote others only in order the better to express myself".

After a couple of years of sticky notes on the fridge, Michelle had a grand idea of making a scrapbook for Christmas with photos she had taken throughout the year, sprinkling in the quotes that she had collected, a tradition that she has carried forward to this day. In 2013, a couple of years after the twins had left for college, I modified the process and started emailing the family five or six quotes at the beginning of each month. With the scrapbooks and the emails, I had access to all the quotes dating back to 2005. The majority of the quotes and notes were intended to influence my children in a positive way at a time in their life when they were making decisions with long-term consequences on the trajectory of their life. Accordingly, the content is heavily focused on topics such as character, wisdom, love and marriage, faith, work, money and success.

For my birthday in 2021, my children gave me a subscription to StoryWorth, which is a website that creates story books. StoryWorth sends me a question every week for a year, which I answer and email back to them. Although at times it feels like I'm writing my obituary, I think it will help avoid a common lament among children whose parents have passed, wishing they had asked more questions while their parents were alive. Several months ago, while in StoryWorth reminiscing mode, I had the idea that I should compile all my quotes and notes in some accessible format for my children, which led to the thought of publishing this book. So if you were kind enough to buy it, I'm very grateful, but selling wasn't my primary focus. On the other hand, I'm genuinely hopeful that this may help you in your parenting journey, or even brighten a day or ease a worry of your own. In any case, I hope you find the book as rewarding to read as I did to write.

J.A.

My first book of quotes, 1974. Copyright 1972
by Word, Incorporated, Waco, TX 76703

Character

> Be at war with your vices, at peace with your neighbors, and let every new year find you a better man.
>
> —BENJAMIN FRANKLIN

Mary, me, and Aubrey, Nashville, 1998

CHARACTER

Discipline yourself so others don't have to.

—JOHN WOODEN

Character is like a tree and reputation like a shadow. The shadow is what we think of it, the tree is the real thing.

—ABRAHAM LINCOLN

Power is the ability to do good things for others.

—BROOKE ASTOR

Storms make oaks take deeper roots.

—GEORGE HERBERT

It takes many good deeds to build a good reputation, and only one bad one to lose it.

—BENJAMIN FRANKLIN

QUOTES & NOTES

No duty is more urgent than
that of returning thanks.

—JAMES ALLEN

Patience is bitter, but its fruit is sweet.

—JEAN-JACQUES ROUSSEAU

Remember that though another may have
more money, beauty, and brains than you,
when it comes to the rare spiritual values such
as charity, self-sacrifice, honor, and nobility,
you have an equal chance with everyone to
be the most beloved and honored of all.

—ARCHIBALD RUTLEDGE

We grow a little every time we do not take
advantage of somebody's weakness.

—BERNARD WILLIAMS

Honesty is the first chapter of the book of wisdom.

—THOMAS JEFFERSON

Ego is the anesthesia that deadens
the pain of stupidity.

—FRANK LEAHY

Conscience is that small still voice that
is sometimes too loud for comfort.

—BERT MURRAY

I don't believe in collective guilt, but I do
believe in collective responsibility.

—AUDREY HEPBURN

What's right is not always popular,
what's popular is not always right.

—ANONYMOUS

In reading the lives of great men, I found that
the first victory they won was over themselves.
Self-discipline with all of them came first.

—HARRY TRUMAN

Life is never easy. There is work to be done
and obligations to be met — obligations
to truth, to justice, and to liberty.

—JOHN F. KENNEDY

You can only be young once, but
you can always be immature.

—JOHN NEELY KENNEDY

Politeness is a small price to pay
for the affection of others.

—ANONYMOUS

> You can't build a reputation on what you're going to do.
>
> —HENRY FORD

Aubrey, Mary, and Alex, Jackson Hole, 2020

There are two freedoms: the false, where one is free to do what he pleases, and the true, where he's free to do what he ought.

—CHARLES KINGSLEY

Forget what you do for others, but don't forget what they do for you.

—ANONYMOUS

People show what they are by what they do with what they have.

—ANONYMOUS

Temper is what gets most of us in trouble. Pride is what keeps us there.

—MARK TWAIN

CHARACTER

Endurance is the art of survival.

—SAIM CHEEDA

The greatest gift we can give to others is a good example.

—ANONYMOUS

The gentle mind by gentle deeds is known. For a person by nothing is so well betrayed as by their manners.

—EDMUND SPENSER

The right to do something does not make doing it right.

—ANONYMOUS

We spend much time in being people
who we wouldn't like to be.

—ANONYMOUS

God gave you a gift of 86,400 seconds today.
Have you used one to say thank you?

—WILLIAM ARTHUR WARD

The greatest of faults...
is to be conscious of none.

—THOMAS CARLYLE

Age is no guarantee of maturity.

—LAWANA BLACKWELL

Even if you're a minority of one,
the truth is still the truth.

—MAHATMA GANDHI

What lies behind us and what lies before us are tiny matters compared to what lies within us.

—RALPH WALDO EMERSON

Aubrey and Mary, Bosphorus, Turkey 2013

QUOTES & NOTES

You can judge the character of a person by how they treat people who can do nothing for them.

—MALCOLM FORBES

There are no persons capable of stooping so low as those who desire to rise in the world.

—MARGUERITE GARDINER

If you don't like something, change it. If you can't change it, change your attitude. Don't complain.

—MAYA ANGELOU

With self-discipline, most anything is possible.

—THEODORE ROOSEVELT

Do you wish to rise? Begin by descending.
You plan a tower that will pierce the clouds?
Lay first the foundation of humility.

—SAINT AUGUSTINE

Fear less, hope more. Eat less, chew more. Whine less, breathe more. Talk less, say more. Hate less, love more, and all good things are yours.

—SWEDISH PROVERB

A lady is a woman who makes a
man act like a gentleman.

—ANONYMOUS

People's minds are changed by
observation, not argument.

—WILL ROGERS

ABRAHAM LINCOLN'S ROAD TO THE WHITE HOUSE

1831　Failed business

1832　Defeated for legislature

1833　Second failed business

1835　Was engaged to be married, fiancée died

1836　Nervous breakdown

1839　Defeated for speaker

1840　Defeated for electorate

1843　Defeated for Congress

1848　Defeated for Congress

1849　Sought job of land officer–rejected

1854　Defeated for United States Senate

1856　Defeated for Vice-Presidential nomination

1858　Defeated again for United States Senate

1860　Elected 16th President of the United States

My father, Lee Austin, Korean War, circa 1950

Courage

urage is grace under pressure.

—ERNEST HEMINGWAY

Success is never final, failure is never fatal. It's courage that counts.

—GEORGE TILTON

Never grow a wishbone where your backbone ought to be.

—CLEMENTINE PADDLEFORD

An army of sheep led by a lion would defeat an army of lions led by a sheep.

—ALEXANDER THE GREAT

One man with courage makes a majority.

—ANDREW JACKSON

Nothing in the world can take the place of persistence. Talent will not—nothing is more common than unsuccessful people with talent. Genius will not—unrewarded genius is almost a proverb. Education will not—the world is full of educated derelicts. Persistence and determination are omnipotent.

—CALVIN COOLIDGE

Never think that you are not good enough. People will take you very much at your own reckoning.

—ANTHONY TROLOPPE

Fear not and stand firm.

—EXODUS 14:13

Courage is found in unlikely places.

—J.R.R. TOLKIEN

You can't steal second base and
keep your foot on first.

—FREDERICK B. WILCOX

Effort and courage are not enough
without purpose and direction.

—JOHN F. KENNEDY

Just do what must be done. This may not
be happiness, but it is greatness.

—GEORGE BERNARD SHAW

Courage. Kindness. Friendship. Character.
These are the qualities that define us as human
beings, and propel us, on occasion, to greatness.

—AUGUST PULLMAN

You have no enemies, you say? Alas, my friend, the boast is poor. He who has mingled in the fray of duty that the brave endure, must have made foes. If you have none, small is the work that you have done. You've hit no traitor on the hip. You've dashed no cup from perjured lip. You've never turned the wrong to right. You've been a coward in the fight.

—CHARLES MACKAY

Some men see things as they are and say why. I dream things that never were and say why not?

—GEORGE BERNARD SHAW

Inaction breeds doubt and fear. Action breeds confidence and courage. If you want to conquer fear, do not sit home and think about it. Go out and get busy.

—DALE CARNEGIE

COURAGE

No one ever told me grief felt so much like fear.

—C. S. LEWIS

Courage doesn't always roar. Sometimes courage is the little voice at the end of the day that says I'll try again tomorrow.

—MARY ANNE RADMACHER

The harder the conflict, the greater the triumph.

—GEORGE WASHINGTON

He who does not hope to win has already lost.

—JOSE OLMEDO

> Courage is resistance to fear, mastery of fear—
> not absence of fear.
>
> —MARK TWAIN

Caribbean Sea, 2009

COURAGE

A journey of a thousand miles
begins with a single step.

—LAO TZU

Courage is fear that has said its prayers.

—DOROTHY BERNARD

Scared is what you're feeling.
Brave is what you're doing.

—EMMA DONAGHUE

All through my life, I have been tested. My
will has been tested, my courage has been
tested, my strength has been tested. Now my
patience and endurance are being tested.

—MUHAMMAD ALI

Fear not for the future, weep not for the past.

—PERCY SHELLEY

It's not about the elimination of fear. Rather it's about the elimination of the feeling that the elimination of fear is necessary before we take the next step.

—ROBIN YOUNG

Every artist was at first an amateur.

—RALPH WALDO EMERSON

Never let your head hang down. Never give up and sit down and grieve. Find another way. And don't pray when it rains if you don't pray when the sun shines.

—SATCHEL PAIGE

COURAGE

He who does nothing makes no mistakes.

—**LUCA PACIOLA**

With enough courage, you can
do without a reputation.

—**MARGARET MITCHELL**

Courage and character are inseparable.

—**ANONYMOUS**

Let fear be a counselor and not a jailer.

—**TONY ROBBINS**

I am wounded, but I am not slain. I
shall lay me down and rest a while,
then I will rise and fight again.

—**SIR ANDREW BARTON**

Do not go where the path may lead, go instead
where there is no path and leave a trail.

—RALPH WALDO EMERSON

We must dare to be great; and we must
realize that greatness is the fruit of toil
and sacrifice and high courage.

—THEODORE ROOSEVELT

There are times in life when a person takes
a flashlight to a soul and inspects himself
for will and courage and spirit... Who
am I? And is that going to be enough?

—ANONYMOUS

COURAGE

A person cannot discover new oceans unless
he has the courage to lose sight of the shore.

—ANONYMOUS

All that is necessary for the triumph of
evil is that good men do nothing.

—ANONYMOUS

Difficulties are supposed to make
us better, not bitter.

—ANONYMOUS

Courage is what it takes to stand up and speak.
Wisdom is what it takes to sit down and listen.

—WINSTON CHURCHILL

Kites rise highest against the wind, not with it.

—WINSTON CHURCHILL

For what matters in life is not whether we receive a round of applause; what matters is whether we have the courage to venture forth despite the uncertainty of acclaim.

—AMOR TOWLES

If you never quit, you can never be defeated.

—ANONYMOUS

COURAGE

The 11th commandment:
Thou shalt not give up.

—ANONYMOUS

Whether you think you can or
think you can't, you're right.

—ANONYMOUS

A ship in harbor is safe, but that is
not what ships are built for.

—JOHN SHEDD

**Lead me to a rock
that is too high.**

—ANONYMOUS

Alex, Jackson Hole, Wyoming, 2020

A CONFEDERATE SOLDIER'S PRAYER

*Author unknown, attributed to a battle-weary
soldier near the end of the Civil War*

I asked God for strength, that I might achieve;

I was made weak, that I might
learn humbly to obey.

I asked for health, that I might do greater things;

I was given infirmity, that I might do better things.

I asked for riches, that I might be happy;

I was given poverty, that I might be wise.

I asked for power, that I might
have the praise of men;

I was given weakness, that I
might feel the need of God.

I asked for all things, that I might enjoy life;

I was given life, that I might enjoy all things.

I got nothing that I asked for, but
everything I hoped for.

Almost despite myself, my unspoken
prayers were answered.

I am among all men most richly blessed.

Michelle, Athens, Greece, 2013

Faith

QUOTES & NOTES

Pray for a good harvest but continue to hoe.

—AMISH PROVERB

If the only prayer you said in your whole life was thank you, that would suffice.

—ANONYMOUS

Grace isn't a little prayer you chant before receiving a meal, it's a way to live.

—JACQUELINE WINSPAR

Live simply, love generously, care deeply, speak kindly, leave the rest to God.

—RONALD REAGAN

Aim at heaven and you will get earth thrown in. Aim at earth and you get neither.

—C. S. LEWIS

In the day of prosperity be joyful, and in the day of adversity consider: God has made one as well as the other.

—ECCLESIASTES 7:14

I shall tell you a great secret my friend. Do not wait for the last judgment, it takes place every day.

—ALBERT CAMUS

If you can think of nothing to give thanks for, then you have a short memory.

—ANONYMOUS

Resolution One: I will live for God. Resolution Two: If no one else does, I still will.

—JONATHAN EDWARDS

Whoever rises from prayer a better man, his prayer is answered.

—GEORGE MEREDITH

Lord, grant that I may always desire more than I can accomplish.

—MICHELANGELO

Call on God, but row away from the rocks.

—INDIAN PROVERB

> **To put yourself in second place is the whole significance of life.**
>
> —ANONYMOUS

Istanbul, Turkey, 2013

QUOTES & NOTES

God, give me sympathy and sense, and help me keep my courage high. God give me calm and confidence and please, a twinkle in my eye.

—ANONYMOUS

Thanksgiving was never meant to
be shut up in a single day.

—ROBERT LINTNER

And what does the Lord require of you?
To act justly and to love mercy and
to walk humbly with your God.

—MICAH 6:8

Whoever is generous to the poor lends to the Lord, and He will repay him for his deed.

—PROVERBS 19:17

The heart of man devises his way, but the Lord directs his steps.

—PROVERBS 16:9

Mary, Crested Butte, Colorado, 2021

I can see how it might be possible for a man to look down upon the earth and be an atheist, but I cannot conceive how a man could look up into the heavens and say there is no God.

—**ABRAHAM LINCOLN**

Costa Rica, 2018

My family at my niece's wedding in Texas, 2013

Michelle's family at twins' christening, Nashville, 1992

Family

QUOTES & NOTES

Family is a life jacket in the stormy sea of life.

—J.K. ROWLING

When all the dust is settled and all the crowds are gone, the things that matter are faith, family, and friends.

—BARBARA BUSH

In truth a family is what you make it. It is made strong, not by number of heads counted at the dinner table, but by the rituals you help family members create, by the memories you share, by the commitment of time, caring, and love you show to one another, and by the hopes for the future you have as individuals and as a unit.

—MARGE KENNEDY

Too often we give children answers to remember rather than problems to solve.

—ROGER LEWIN

A mom's hugs last a long time after she lets go.

—ANONYMOUS

If you have a mom there is no where you are likely to go where prayer has not already been.

—ROBERT BRAULT

The kids and Michelle's mom Polly, en route to
Oklahoma for Thanksgiving, 2008

*A child, like your stomach,
doesn't need all you can
afford to give it.*

—FRANK CLARK

The surest way to make it hard for your
children is to make it soft for them.

—ANONYMOUS

A spoiled child never loves his mother.

—ANONYMOUS

Choices... decisions... consequences

—ANONYMOUS

When parents do too much for their children,
the children will not do much for themselves.

—ANONYMOUS

QUOTES & NOTES

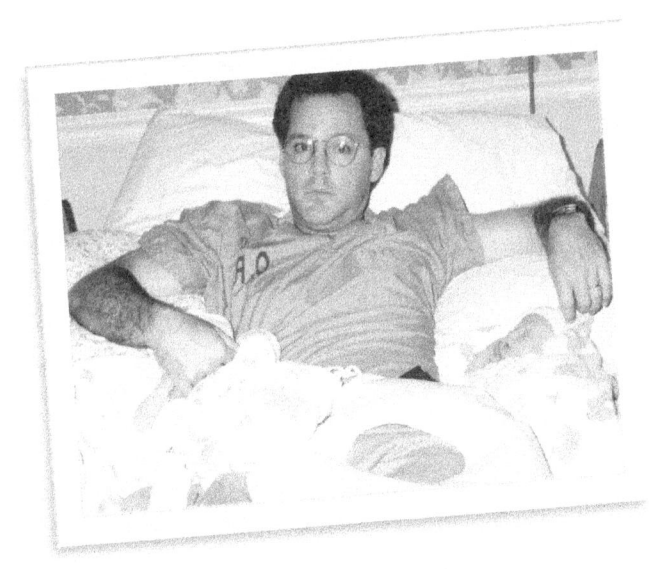

Birth of twins, Baptist Hospital, 1992

Too many people treat parenting like it's the 20th item on their to-do list.

—**JOHN NEELY KENNEDY**

FAMILY

If you can't get along with your brothers and sisters, you won't get along with your friends. If you can't get along with your friends, you won't get along with your classmates. If you can't get along with your family, friends, and classmates, who do you think you CAN get along with?

—ANONYMOUS

If you only have one smile in you, give it to the people you love. Don't be surly at home, then go out in the street and start grinning "Good morning" at total strangers.

—MAYA ANGELOU

He that troubleth his own house shall inherit the wind.

—PROVERBS 11:29

There is no doubt that it is around the family and the home that all the greatest virtues, the most dominating virtues of humans are created, strengthened and maintained.

—WINSTON S. CHURCHILL

Where we love is home. Home that our feet may leave, but not our hearts.

—OLIVER WENDELL HOLMES

The world doesn't love you like your family loves you.

—ANONYMOUS

Families are like branches on a tree. We grow in different directions yet our roots remain as one.

—ANONYMOUS

Don't confuse your children by mixing good counsel with bad conduct.

—ANONYMOUS

Good family is never an accident, but always an achievement by those who share it.

—ANONYMOUS

A family doesn't have to be perfect; it just needs to be united.

—ANONYMOUS

Mount of Olives, Jerusalem, 2018

FAMILY

If you can't do anything with your kids, it's probably because you don't.

—**ANONYMOUS**

Friends, Nashville 2014

Golfing buddies, Nashville 2017

Friendship

Friends are the family you choose for yourself.

—EDNA BUCHANAN

No man is a failure who has friends.

**—"IT'S A WONDERFUL LIFE", 1946.
DIRECTED BY FRANK CAPRA,
PRODUCTION COMPANY LIBERTY FILMS**

Good friends, like good books, should
be few and well chosen.

—CHARLES CALEB COLTON

You don't luck into things as much as you'd
like to think. You build step by step, whether
it's friendships or opportunities.

—BARBARA BUSH

Gotta be a friend to have a friend.

—ANONYMOUS

Boys walking to school, Dar es Salaam, Tanzania, Africa 2017

QUOTES & NOTES

Advice from your friends is like the weather,
some of it is good and some of it is bad.

—ARNOLD LOBEL

Hold a true friend with both your hands.

—AFRICAN PROVERB

When you betray someone else,
you also betray yourself.

—ISAAC BESHEVIS

> There's no friends
> like old friends.
>
> —JAMES JOYCE

Asheville, North Carolina, 1992

If you want to win friends, make it a point to remember them. If you remember my name, you pay me a subtle compliment. You indicate that I have made an impression on you, and add to my feeling of importance.

—DALE CARNEGIE

True friendship is like good health, the value of it is seldom known until it is lost.

—CHARLES CALEB COLTON

It is a good thing to be rich and a good thing to be strong, but it is a better thing to be loved by many friends.

—EURIPIDES

The true friend is the greatest of all blessings, and that which we take the least care of all to acquire.

—FRANCOIS DE LA ROCHEFOUCAULD

If you want an accounting of your worth, count your friends.

—MARY BROWNE

A friend is someone who goes around saying nice things about you behind your back.

—RALPH WALDO EMERSON

Friendship is like money, easier made than kept.

—SAMUEL BUTLER

The surest way to lose a friend is to tell him something for his own good.

—ANONYMOUS

A real friend is one who walks in when the rest of the world walks out.

—WALTER WINCHELL

A friend is someone who can sing you the song of your heart when you've forgotten it.

—ANONYMOUS

FRIENDSHIP

Laughter is the closest distance
between two people.

—VICTOR BORGE

The best antiques are old friends.

—ANONYMOUS

The greedy one stores all but friendship.

—ANONYMOUS

A good friend is like a four leaf clover,
hard to find and lucky to have.

—IRISH PROVERB

My children, niece and nephews, Christmas
morning in Nashville 2006

Happiness

QUOTES & NOTES

Happiness is as a butterfly which, when pursued,
is always beyond our grasp, but which if you
will sit down quietly, may alight upon you.

—NATHANIEL HAWTHORNE

A smile is an inexpensive way
to improve your looks.

—CHARLES GORDY

The secret of happiness is to count your blessings
while others are adding up their troubles.

—WILLIAM PENN

Happiness equals expectations minus reality.

—TOM MAGLIOZZI

Happiness seems made to be shared.

—PIERRE CORNEILLE

Alex, Mary and Aubrey, Athens, Greece, 2013

Unhappiness is not knowing what we
want and killing ourselves to get it.

—DON HEROLD

Happiness is in doing, in accepting, meeting and
conquering the challenges of your life, and where
possible, in doing for others, not for yourself.

—ANONYMOUS

Happiness makes everyone beautiful.

—ANONYMOUS

Laughter is the universal language. It means joy
and gladness, and needs no further interpretation.

—ANONYMOUS

HAPPINESS

People can only be happy when they do not assume that the object of life is happiness.

—GEORGE ORWELL

A smile is a curve that can set a lot of things straight.

—PHYLLIS DILLER

Happiness is not our destination but our mode of transportation.

—ROY GOODMAN

To be truly happy you must have three things: someone to love, something to do, and something to hope for.

—TOM BODETT

Photo booth at my son's wedding, Miami, 2022
with my two daughters' boyfriends

Humorous

Those who spend the day boasting about
the wonderful things they plan to do
probably did the same thing yesterday.

—ANONYMOUS

Genius may have its limitations, but
stupidity is not thus handicapped.

—ELBERT HUBBARD

People say I'm indecisive. [dramatic pause]
Well I just don't know about that...

—GEORGE H. W. BUSH

Blessed is the man who can laugh at himself,
for he will never cease to be amused.

—H. L. MENCKEN

> **Always put off 'til tomorrow what you shouldn't do at all.**
>
> —ANONYMOUS

New Year's Resolution: To tolerate fools more gladly, provided this does not encourage them to take up more of my time.

—JAMES AGATE

Always follow your heart... but take your brains with you.

—JOHN NEELY KENNEDY

Why not go out on a limb? Isn't that where the fruit is?

—MARK TWAIN

I always advise people never to give advice.

—P.G. WODEHOUSE

The confidence of ignorance will
always overcome indecision.

—DAVID STOREY

Worry is like a rocking chair. It gives you
something to do, but it doesn't get you anywhere.

—VAN WILDER

Live in such a way that you wouldn't be ashamed
to sell your parrot to the town gossip

—WILL ROGERS

QUOTES & NOTES

However beautiful the strategy, you
should occasionally look at the results.

—WINSTON CHURCHILL

Always go to other people's funerals,
otherwise they won't come to yours.

—YOGI BERRA

All things come to those who wait, but sometimes
it's just the leftovers from who got there first.

—ANONYMOUS

Common sense is like deodorant. The
people who need it most never use it.

—ANONYMOUS

Getting mad is like wetting your pants. Everybody sees it, but you're the only one that feels it.

—ANONYMOUS

More wag, less bark.

—ANONYMOUS

There's three kinds of people in the world: those who make things happen, those to whom things happen, and those who say what just happened.

—ANONYMOUS

If people don't want to come out to the ballpark, nobody's going to stop them.

—YOGI BERRA

QUOTES & NOTES

Tomorrow is often the busiest day of the year.

—ANONYMOUS

There are seven days in a week and
someday is not one of them.

—BENNY LEWIS

If plan A fails,
remember you have 25 more letters.

—CHRIS GUILLEBEAU

When you reach for the stars, you may
not quite get them, but you won't come
up with a handful of mud either.

—LEO BURNETT

Hitchhiker, Uganda, 2018

THE MAN IN THE ARENA

"It is not the critic who counts; not the man who points out how the strong man stumbles, or where the doer of deeds could have done them better. The credit belongs to the man who is actually in the arena, whose face is marred by dust and sweat and blood; who strives valiantly; who errs, who comes short again and again, because there is no effort without error and shortcoming; but who does actually strive to do the deeds; who knows great enthusiasms, the great devotions; who spends himself in a worthy cause; who at the best knows in the end the triumph of high achievement, and who at the worst, if he fails, at least fails while daring greatly, so that his place shall never be with those cold and timid souls who neither know victory nor defeat."

—THEODORE ROOSEVELT
APRIL 23, 1910

Leadership

> Nobody cares how much you know until they know how much you care.
>
> —THEODORE ROOSEVELT

Uganda, 2018

LEADERSHIP

People cannot be managed. Inventories can be managed, but people must be led.

—ROSS PEROT

Lead, follow, or get out of the way.

—THOMAS PAINE

The true leader is always led.

—CARL JUNG

Consider the rights of others before your own feelings, and the feelings of others before your own rights.

—JOHN WOODEN

You can't let praise or criticism get to you. It's
a weakness to get caught up in either one.

—JOHN WOODEN

It's amazing what you can accomplish
if no one cares who gets the credit.

—HARRY S. TRUMAN

I'VE LEARNED

I've learned... That the best classroom in the world is at the feet of an elderly person.

I've learned... That when you're in love, it shows.

I've learned... That just one person saying to me, 'You've made my day!' makes my day.

I've learned... That having a child fall asleep in your arms is one of the most peaceful feelings in the world.

I've learned... That being kind is more important than being right.

I've learned... That I can always pray for someone when I don't have the strength to help him in any other way.

I've learned... That no matter how serious your life requires you to be, everyone needs a friend to act goofy with.

I've learned. . . That simple walks with my father around the block on summer nights when I was a child did wonders for me as an adult.

I've learned. . . That life is like a roll of toilet paper. The closer it gets to the end, the faster it goes.

I've learned. . . That we should be glad God doesn't give us everything we ask for.

I've learned. . . That money doesn't buy class.

I've learned. . . That under everyone's hard shell is someone who wants to be appreciated and loved.

I've learned. . . That to ignore the facts does not change the facts.

I've learned. . . That when you plan to get even with someone, you are only letting that person continue to hurt you.

I've learned. . . That the easiest way for me to grow as a person is to surround myself with people smarter than I am.

I've learned. . . That everyone you meet deserves to be greeted with a smile.

I've learned... That opportunities are never lost; someone will take the ones you miss.

I've learned... That when you harbor bitterness, happiness will dock elsewhere.

I've learned... That one should keep his words both soft and tender, because tomorrow he may have to eat them.

I've learned... That a smile is an inexpensive way to improve your looks.

I've learned... That the less time I have to work with, the more things I get done.

I've learned... That everyone wants to live on top of the mountain, but all the happiness and growth occurs while you're climbing it.

—ANDY ROONEY, 1919-2011
CBS NEWS CORRESPONDENT

Alex, Mary, Aubrey, and Alex's wife Mallory,
Miami, Florida, 2019

Life

QUOTES & NOTES

Until you are at peace with who you are, you'll never be at peace with what you have.

—DORIS MORTMAN

People who say it cannot be done should not interrupt those who are doing it.

—GEORGE BERNARD SHAW

There is more to life than increasing its speed.

—MAHATMA GANDHI

Never waste a minute thinking about people you don't like.

—DWIGHT D. EISENHOWER

We travel this road but once, but if we play our cards right, once is enough.

—FRANK SINATRA

Time moves slowly, but passes quickly.

—ALICE WALKER

The Astronomical Clock (and my Timex),
Prague, Czechoslovakia 2016

If you believe something then you will live it, if you don't live it, then you don't really believe it.

—ANONYMOUS

Let disappointment be your inspiration.

—ANONYMOUS

Those who never make mistakes
never make anything.

—ALBERT EINSTEIN

Play so that you may be serious.

—ANACHARSIS

It does not matter how slow you go
so long as you do not stop.

—CONFUCIUS

Experience is a hard teacher. She tests
first and teaches afterwards.

- VERNON LAW

Small opportunities are often the
beginning of great enterprises.

—DEMOSTHENES

Trees often transplanted seldom prosper.

—DUTCH PROVERB

Some things are best mended by a break.

—EDITH WHARTON

Some days there won't be a song
in your heart. Sing anyway.

—EMORY AUSTIN

Architecture is frozen music.

—FRANK LLOYD WRIGHT

Sagrada Familia, Barcelona, Spain, 2014

This too shall pass.

— HAKIM SANAI

The best and most beautiful things in life cannot
be seen, not touched, but are felt in the heart.

—HELEN KELLER

One often meets his destiny on
the road he takes to avoid it.

—JEAN DE LA FONTAINE

Inaction can be the biggest form of action.

—JERRY BROWN

Vision without purpose is only a dream.

—JOEL BARKER

Try and fail, but don't fail to try.

—JOHN QUINCY ADAMS

Things turn out for the best for the people who make the best of the way things turn out.

—JOHN WOODEN

As a rule, what is out of sight disturbs people's minds more seriously than what they see.

—JULIUS CAESAR

Dance as if no one's watching, sing as if no one's listening, and live everyday as if it were your last.

—KATHRYN SHAY

To be able to look back upon one's life in satisfaction, is to live twice.

—KHALIL GIBRAN

I've got a theory that if you give 100% all the time, somehow things will work out in the end.

—LARRY BIRD

Iron rusts from disuse; stagnant water loses its purity and in cold weather becomes frozen; even so does inaction sap the vigor of the mind.

—LEONARDO DA VINCI

Read aggressively.

—ANONYMOUS

If you're bored with life, and you don't get up every morning with a burning desire to do things, you don't have enough goals.

—LOU HOLTZ

He who is outside his door has the hardest
part of his journey behind him.

—FLEMISH PROVERB

Wrinkles should merely indicate
where the smiles have been.

—MARK TWAIN

Enjoy your own life without comparing
it with that of another.

—MARQUIS DE CONDORCET

Nothing fixes a thing so intensely in the
memory as the wish to forget it.

—MICHEL DE MONTAIGNE

A goal is a dream with a deadline.

—NAPOLEAN HILL

Without music, life is a journey through the desert.

—PAT CONROY

The best things in life aren't things.

—PEGGY ANDERSON

An ounce of accomplishment is
worth a ton of good intentions.

—RALPH WALDO EMERSON

The chains of habit are too weak to be
felt yet too strong to be broken.

—SAMUEL JOHNSON

Life is like a grindstone. Whether it
grinds you down or polishes you depends
on the stuff you are made of.

—THOMAS HOLDCROFT

> There are flowers everywhere, for those who bother to look.
>
> —HENRI MATISSE

Mary and Michelle, Crested Butte, Colorado, 2021

Every exit is an entrance somewhere else.

—TOM STOPPARD

Even if you're on the right track, you'll
get run over if you just sit there.

—WILL ROGERS

Continuous effort, not strength or intelligence,
is the key to unlocking our potential.

—WINSTON CHURCHILL

If you're going through hell, keep going.

—WINSTON CHURCHILL

An opportunity grasped and used produces
at least one other opportunity.

—ANONYMOUS

QUOTES & NOTES

Do not squander time, it is the
stuff that life is made of.

—ANONYMOUS

Falling down is part of life.
Getting back up is living.

—ANONYMOUS

I have no yesterdays, time took them away.
Tomorrow may not be, but I have today.

—ANONYMOUS

If your life takes a turn for the worse,
remember that you're the one who's driving.

—ANONYMOUS

Slow and steady wins the race.

—ANONYMOUS

It is not good to have too much liberty. It
is not good to have all one wants.

—ANONYMOUS

Life consists not in holding good cards
but in playing those you hold well.

—ANONYMOUS

Life is the art of drawing sufficient
conclusions from insufficient premises.

—ANONYMOUS

One trouble with trouble is that it
usually starts out like fun.

—ANONYMOUS

The path of least resistance is always downhill.

—ANONYMOUS

Sometimes those moments that you spend hoping
and believing and waiting for something good
to happen are the best moments of your life.

—ANONYMOUS

Only the second rate are safe
from the jealousy of others.

—ANONYMOUS

Slow and steady wins the race.

—ANONYMOUS

The oil of courtesy will reduce a lot of friction.

—ANONYMOUS

When I grow up, I want to be a little boy.

—JOSEPH HELLE

Alex, in Nashville, 1996

The ones that have the luck are always ones that don't depend on it.

—ANONYMOUS

Too much freedom is its own kind of cage.

—ANONYMOUS

What is life but to dream and do.

—ANONYMOUS

When you stop giving, you stop living.

—ANONYMOUS

The most consummately beautiful thing in the universe is a rightly fashioned life of a good person.

—GEORGE HERBERT PALMER

> On matters of style,
> swim with the current,
> on matters of principle,
> stand like a rock.
>
> —THOMAS JEFFERSON

Acuwa River, Uganda, 2018

QUOTES & NOTES

People that worry the most have
the most time to worry.

—ANONYMOUS

All the flowers of tomorrow are
in the seeds of today.

—INDIAN PROVERB

How empty is the life that is
filled only with things.

—ANONYMOUS

Part of getting over it is knowing
you may never get over it.

—ANONYMOUS

> Life is a great big canvas, throw all the paint you can at it.
>
> —ANONYMOUS

Lennon Wall, Prague, Czech Republic 2015

Mary, Aubrey, Alex, Nashville, 1998

Love

The love we give away is the only love we keep.

—ELBERT HUBBARD

Immature love says I love you because I need you.
Mature love says I need you because I love you.

—ERICH FROMM

Pride makes us do things well. But it is love
that makes us do them to perfection.

—H. JACKSON BROWN, JR.

Fragrance always stays in the
hand that gives the rose.

—HADA BEJAR

Love is friendship
set on fire.

—JEREMY TAYLOR

Alex and Mallory, Santa Rosa Beach, Florida, 2016

People are unreasonable, illogical, and
self-centered. Love them anyway.

—MOTHER TERESA

No one worth possessing can be quite possessed.

—SARA TEASDALE

Treasure the love you receive above
all. It will survive long after your gold
and good health have vanished.

—ANONYMOUS

We cannot all do great things, but we
can do small things with great love.

—ANONYMOUS

Love is when the other person's happiness
is more important than your own.

—H. JACKSON BROWN, JR.

Saint Barthelemy, 2012

Love and Forgiveness

Forgiveness is a funny thing. It warms the heart and cools the sting.

—WILLIAM ARTHUR WARD

One of the secrets of a long and fruitful life is to forgive everybody everything every night before you go to bed.

—BERNARD BARUCH

To err is human, to forgive, infrequent.

—ANONYMOUS

There is no love without forgiveness, and there is no forgiveness without love.

—BRYANT H. MCGILL

The weak can never forgive. Forgiveness
is the attribute of the strong.

—MAHATMA GANDHI

To err is human, to forgive divine.

—ALEXANDER POPE

The more a person knows, the more they forgive.

—CONFUCIUS

Life is an adventure in forgiveness.

—NORMAN COUSINS

Without forgiveness life is governed by an
endless cycle of resentment and retaliation.

—ROBERT ASSAGIOLI

Medical Mission, Dar es Salaam, Tanzania, Africa 2017

Love and Kindness

Always be a little kinder than necessary.

—JAMES M. BARRIE

No act of kindness, no matter
how small, is ever wasted.

—AESOP

It's nice to be important but it's
more important to be nice.

—JOHN TEMPLETON

Kind words do not cost much. They never blister
the tongue or lips. They make other people good-
natured. They also produce their own image
on men's souls, and a beautiful image it is.

—BLAISE PASCAL

Neither fire nor wind, birth nor death
can erase our good deeds.

—BUDDHA

There are no unimportant jobs, no unimportant
people, no unimportant acts of kindness.

—ANONYMOUS

And what does the Lord require of you
but to do justice, and to love kindness,
and to walk humbly with your God?

—MICAH 6:8

Sympathy is the first condition of criticism.

—HENRI AMIEL

Nothing soothes pain like human touch.

—BOBBY FISCHER

> Be kind, for everyone you meet is fighting a hard battle.
>
> —IAN MCCLAREN

Alex, camp counselor, Monterey, TN, 2014

Have a heart that never hardens, a temper
that never tires, a touch that never hurts.

—CHARLES DICKENS

You cannot do a kindness too soon, for you
never know how soon it will be too late.

—RALPH WALDO EMERSON

Kind words can be short and easy to speak,
but their echoes are truly endless.

—SARAH RAANAN

How far you go in life depends on your being
tender with the young, compassionate with the
aged, sympathetic with the striving, and tolerant
of the weak and strong. Because someday in
your life you will have been all of these.

—GEORGE WASHINGTON CARVER

Michelle and me, South Carolina, 2015

Love and Marriage

To keep a fire burning brightly there's one easy rule: keep the two logs together, near enough to keep each other warm and far enough apart—a finger's breadth— for breathing room. Good fire, good marriage, same rule.

—ANONYMOUS

Michelle and me, Costa Rica, 2018

In a time when nothing is more certain than change, the commitment of two people to one another has become difficult and rare. Yet by its scarcity, the beauty and value of this exchange have only been enhanced.

—ROBERT SEXTON

Marriage is like a tree; sometimes in bud, sometimes in blossom, sometimes in leaf, sometimes in fruit. Sometimes leaves will fall off and it will look bare, but if you keep cultivating the roots it will come alive again.

—ANONYMOUS

Grow old with me. The best is yet to be.

—MARY CHAPIN CARPENTER

For where you go I will go, and where you lodge I will lodge. Your people shall be my people, and your God my God. Where you die I will die, and there will I be buried. May the Lord do so to me and more also if anything but death parts me from you.

—RUTH 2:16-17

The value of marriage is not that adults produce children, but that children produce adults.

—PETER DEVRIES

Men are like wine. Some turn to vinegar, the best improve with age.

—POPE JOHN XIII

A broken home is the world's greatest wreck.

—ANONYMOUS

LOVE AND MARRIAGE

Love is when two people join together and make each other better for having the other in their life.

—ANONYMOUS

Often a good marriage depends on
leaving a few things a day left unsaid.

—ANONYMOUS

The girls in Paris

Money

Annual income twenty pounds, annual expenditure nineteen pounds, result happiness. Annual income 19 pounds, annual expenditure 20, result misery.

—CHARLES DICKENS

The idea is to make a little money first, then make a little money last.

—ANONYMOUS

A fool and his money are soon parted.

—ENGLISH PROVERB

Contentment comes not from riches but from simple wants.

—EPICTETUS

Money doesn't make you happy,
but it does quiet the nerves.

—SEAN O'CASEY

Buy land. They ain't making any more of the stuff.

—WILL ROGERS

It is not in riches that we find contentment,
but in contentment that we find riches.

—ANONYMOUS

Too many people spend money they
haven't earned to buy things they don't
want to impress people they don't like.

—WILL ROGERS

To have enough is good luck, to have more than enough is harmful. This is true of all things, but especially of money.

—ANONYMOUS

Waste not, want not.

—ANONYMOUS

Most people don't spend more than they earn. They just spend it quicker than they earn it.

—ANONYMOUS

THE BIXBY LETTER

Executive Mansion,
Washington, Nov. 21, 1864.
Dear Madam,

I have been shown in the files of the War Department a statement of the Adjutant General of Massachusetts that you are the mother of five sons who have died gloriously on the field of battle.

I feel how weak and fruitless must be any words of mine which should attempt to beguile you from the grief of a loss so overwhelming. But I cannot refrain from tendering to you the consolation that may be found in the thanks of the Republic they died to save.

I pray that our Heavenly Father may assuage the anguish of your bereavement, and leave you only the cherished memory of the loved and lost, and the solemn pride that must be yours to have laid so costly a sacrifice upon the altar of Freedom.

Yours, very sincerely and respectfully,
   A. Lincoln

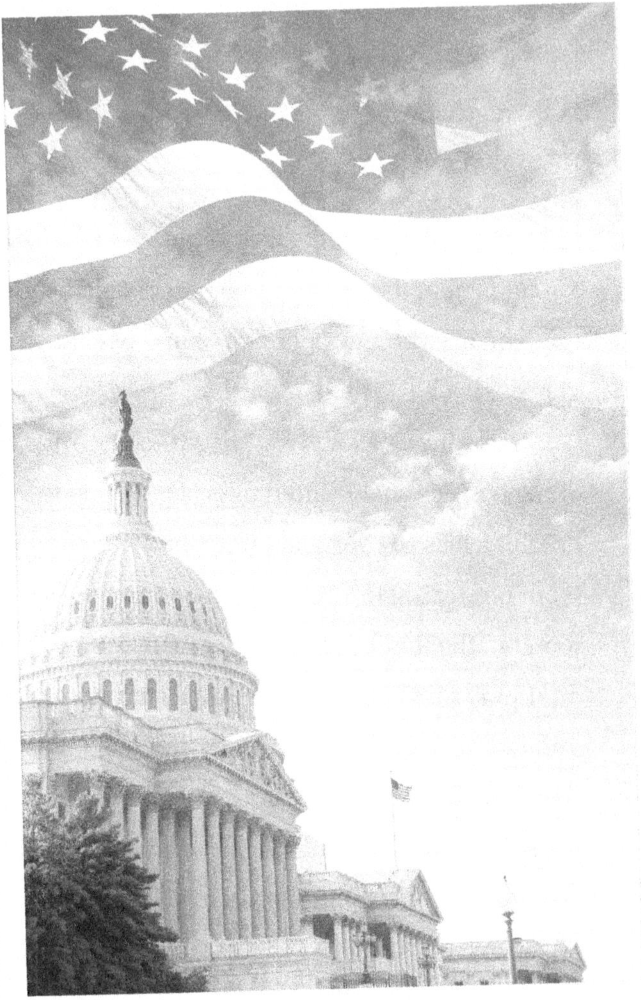

Politics

> The integrity of a nation is best judged by how it takes care of its elderly, its handicapped, its sick, and its children.
>
> —ANONYMOUS

National Children's Hospital, Bishkek, Kyrgyzstan, 2016

My fellow Americans, ask not what
your country can do for you, ask what
you can do for your country.

—JOHN F. KENNEDY

A people that values its privileges above
its principles soon loses both.

—DWIGHT D. EISENHOWER

Sometimes the majority just means
all the fools are on the same side.

—JOHN NEELY KENNEDY

A fool and his money are soon elected.

—WILL ROGERS

If you believe that tax policy has nothing to do with the economy, then you're pretty much like a rock, only dumber.

—JOHN NEELY KENNEDY

A politician is someone who can make waves and then convince you he is the only one who can save the ship.

—ANONYMOUS

> If we do not believe in freedom of speech for those we despise, we do not believe in it at all.
>
> —NOAM CHOMSKY

Nashville Tennessee, 2021

Dinner with friends, Nashville, 2016

ND Word

Four things come not back: the spoken word, the spent arrow, the past, and the neglected opportunity.

—ARABIAN PROVERB

If you are accomplished, people will talk about it for you. You don't have to point it out.

—ANONYMOUS

The liar's punishment is not in the least that he is not believed, but that he cannot believe anyone else.

—GEORGE BERNARD SHAW

A closed mouth gathers no foot.

—BARRY POPIK

Always tell the truth and you won't
have to remember what you said.

—MARK TWAIN

Be fascinating, maybe even
controversial, but never polarizing.

—ANONYMOUS

If you want people to think well of
you, do not speak well of yourself.

—BLAISE PASCAL

Beware of a narrow mind with a wide mouth.

—CELIA GREEN

Lying to ourselves is more deeply
ingrained than lying to others.

—DOSTOYEVSKY

QUOTES & NOTES

Silence is one of the great arts of conversation.

—CICERO

True words are not always pretty,
pretty words are not always true.

—FRANK MOHANNA

Promise is most given when the least is said.

—GEORGE CHAPMAN

Blessed is the man who, having nothing to say,
abstains from giving us wordy evidence of the fact.

—GEORGE ELIOT

A jest often decides matters of importance more effectually and happily than seriousness.

—HORACE

Hydra, Greece, 2019

Silence. One of the hardest arguments to refute.

—JOSH BILLINGS

The more you talk the less people listen.

—MEG WHITE

Gossip, unlike river water, flows both ways.

—MICHAEL KORDA

I quote others only in order the
better to express myself.

—MONTAIGNE

Do not say a little in many words
but a great deal in a few.

—PYTHAGORUS

The vanity of being known to be
trusted with a secret is generally one
of the chief motives to disclose it.

—SAMUEL JOHNSON

Whoever gossips to you will gossip about you.

—SPANISH PROVERB

One of the lessons of history is that
nothing is often a good thing to do
and always a good thing to say.

—WILL DURANT

How you say it can be as
important as what you say.

—ANONYMOUS

It's a fine thing to be honest, but it is
also very important to be right.

—WINSTON CHURCHILL

It's difficult to keep quiet
if you have nothing to say.

—ANONYMOUS

The only time people dislike gossip
is when you gossip about them.

—ANONYMOUS

Those who say don't know, those
who know don't say.

—LAO TZU

Don't talk unless you can improve the silence.

—JORGE LUIS BORGES

Even a fish wouldn't get caught if it kept its mouth shut.

—ANONYMOUS

Abigail and Lady, Nashville, 2018

Church baseball, Memphis, 1964. I'm front
left, my brother Jim next to me.

Golfing in California, 2016

Sports

Coach with answers, not volume.

—ANONYMOUS

The main ingredient of stardom
is the rest of the team.

—JOHN WOODEN

When the Great scorer comes to write against your name, he marks not that you won or lost, but how you played the game.

—GRANTLAND RICE

Winning takes talent, to repeat takes character.

—JOHN WOODEN

SPORTS

If it's close, swing the bat.

—ANONYMOUS

You always miss 100%
of the shots you don't take.

—WAYNE GRETZKY

How you win shows some of your
character, how you lose shows all of it.

—BART STARR

QUOTES & NOTES

One person practicing sportsmanship is better than fifty preaching it.

—KNUTE ROCKNE

Rick Byrd, Belmont basketball head coach, Fort Worth, Texas, 2017

Dad, Aubrey, and Alex all graduating the same day, Athens, Georgia, 2015

Success

Success is becoming the best that
you are capable of becoming.

—JOHN WOODEN

Nothing fails like success, nothing
succeeds like failure.

—MARGARET DRABBLE

Always bear in mind that your own
resolution to succeed is more important
than any other one thing.

—ABRAHAM LINCOLN

If you want your dreams to come true, don't oversleep.

—NICKY GUMBEL

Sunrise, Pebble Beach, California, 2012

Sorrento, Italy, 2015

SUCCESS

That man is a success who has lived well, laughed often, and loved much; who has gained the respect of intelligent men and the love of children; who has filled his niche and accomplished his task; who leaves the world better than he found it; who never lacked appreciation of the Earth's beauty or failed to express it; who looked for the best in others and gave the best he had.

—ROBERT LOUIS STEVENSON

No formula for success will work if you don't.

—ANONYMOUS

Success is one percent inspiration
and 99 percent perspiration

—THOMAS EDISON

Show me a thoroughly satisfied man
and I'll show you a failure.

—THOMAS EDISON

Success usually comes to those who
are too busy to be looking for it.

—HENRY DAVID THOREAU

The wind and the waves are always on the side of the ablest navigators.

—EDWARD GIBBON

French Riviera 2012

It takes 20 years to make an overnight success.

—EDDIE CANTOR

Success does not consist in never making mistakes
but in never making the same one a second time.

—GEORGE BERNARD SHAW

Difficulties mastered are opportunities won.

—WINSTON CHURCHILL

The sure way to succeed is to
endure to the very end.

—ANONYMOUS

There's no great pleasure in achieving success
if nothing ever stood in the way of it.

—ANONYMOUS

The world steps aside for those who
know where they are going.

—JAMES ALLEN

You only have to be 10% better at
what you do to go 100% further.

—ANONYMOUS

The person who makes a success of living
is the one who sees his goal steadily
and aims for it unswervingly.

—CECIL B. DEMILLE

The man who claims he never made a mistake
in his life generally has a wife who did.

—ANONYMOUS

Failure is instructive. The person who
really thinks learns quite as much from
his failures as from his successes.

—JOHN DEWEY

SUCCESS

If you want to be successful, it's as simple as this: know what you're doing, love what you're doing, and believe in what you're doing.

—**WILL ROGERS**

Medical Mission, Bishkek, Kyrgyzstan
2016 with interpreter Tynys

Wisdom

Few people have the natural strength to honor a friend's success without envy.

—AESCHYLUS

Hope for the best, plan for the worst. Hope is not a plan.

—ANONYMOUS

Everything in life should be made as simple as possible, but not simpler.

—ALBERT EINSTEIN

Vision without action is a daydream. Action without vision is nightmare.

—JAPANESE PROVERB

To do two things at once is to do neither.

—PUBLILIUS SYRUS

The best remedy for anger is delay.

—SENECA

Correlation is not causation.

—ANONYMOUS

If the only tool you have is a hammer every problem looks like a nail.

—ABRAHAM MASLOV

Next to knowing when to seize an opportunity, the next important thing is to know when to forego an advantage.

—BENJAMIN DISRAELI

One of the hardest things in life to learn is which bridge to cross and which bridge to burn.

—DAVID RUSSELL

Michelle, Mary, Aubrey, and Alex, Pont du Gard, Les Angeles, France 2017

WISDOM

A good solution applied with vigor now is better than a perfect solution applied 10 minutes later.

—GEN. GEORGE S. PATTON

Several excuses are always less convincing than one.

—ALDOUS HUXLEY 1928

If you don't stand for something, you'll fall for anything.

—ALEXANDER HAMILTON

Choice, not chance, determines your destiny.

—ARISTOTLE

Nothing is a waste of time if you use the experience wisely.

—AUGUST RODIN

Don't waste time looking for shortcuts
to any place worth going.

—BEVERLY SILLS

He who asks may be a fool for five minutes, but
he who does not ask remains a fool forever.

—CHINESE PROVERB

If you're patient in one moment of anger,
you will escape a hundred days of sorrow.

—CHINESE PROVERB

Never insult an alligator until
you've crossed the river.

—CORDELL HULL

When I was a child, I spoke like a child, I thought like a child, I reasoned like a child. When I became a man, I gave up childish ways.

—CORINTHIANS 13:11

Experience has two things to teach, the first is we must correct a great deal, The second is we must not correct too much.

— DELACROIX

You have brains in your head. You have feet in your shoes. You can steer yourself in any direction you choose.

—DR. SEUSS

Learn from others' mistakes. You won't live long enough to make them all yourself.

—ELEANOR ROOSEVELT

It takes as much energy to wish as it does to plan.

—ELEANOR ROOSEVELT

He who angers you conquers you.

—ELIZABETH KENNY

The bitterness of studying is preferable
to the bitterness of ignorance.

—FILIPINO PROVERB

Beware of false knowledge; it is more
dangerous than ignorance.

—GEORGE BERNARD SHAW

The moment we want to believe something,
we suddenly see all the arguments for it, and
become blind to the arguments against it.

—GEORGE BERNARD SHAW

Cursing the weather is never good farming.

—ENGLISH PROVERB

Tact is the art of making a point
without making an enemy.

—ISAAC NEWTON

The best armor is to keep out of range.

—ITALIAN PROVERB

You ain't gonna learn from what
you don't wanna know.

—JERRY GARCIA

A man must be big enough to admit his
mistakes, smart enough to profit from them,
and strong enough to correct them.

—JOHN C. MAXWELL

To handle yourself use your head, to handle others use your heart.

—ELEANOR ROOSEVELT

When people are least sure they are most dogmatic.

—JOHN KENNETH GALBRAITH

As scarce as truth is, the supply has always exceeded the demand.

—JOSH BILLINGS

All wish to possess knowledge, but few, comparatively speaking, are willing to pay the price.

—JUVENAL

Don't outsmart your common sense.

—LEE BRICE

It is a bad plan that admits to no modification.

—PUBLILIUS SYRUS

You can't dispel ignorance if you retain arrogance.

—RICHARD BARONE

The easiest person to deceive is yourself.

—RICHARD FEYNMAN

Better to be ignorant of a matter
than to half know it.

—PUBLILIUS SYRUS

Doing your best at this moment puts you
in the best place for the next moment.

—OPRAH WINFREY

Advice is like snow, the softer it
falls, the deeper it goes.

—SAMUEL COLERIDGE

I have noted that persons with bad judgment are
most insistent that we do what they think best.

—LIONEL ABEL

Those who will not reason are bigots; those who
cannot are fools; those who dare not are slaves.

—LORD BYRON

> Be wiser than other people, if you can, but do not tell them so.
>
> —PHILIP STANHOPE

A present from work colleagues in Nebraska, 2017

No man is wise enough by himself.

—TITUS MACCIUS PLAUTUS

Aubrey and Alex, Caesarea, Israel, 2018

WISDOM

Integrity without knowledge is weak and useless, and knowledge without integrity is dangerous and dreadful.

—SAMUEL JOHNSON

I wasted time, and now time doth waste me.

—SHAKESPEARE

Don't throw away the old bucket until you know whether the new one holds water.

—SWEDISH PROVERB

To show resentment at a reproach is to acknowledge that one may have deserved it.

—TACITUS

QUOTES & NOTES

It is a great mistake to think you are more than you are, and yet to underestimate your real value.

—THOMAS CARLYLE

The best thinking is done in solitude,
the worst is done in turmoil.

—THOMAS EDISON

You can't direct the wind, but
you can adjust the sails.

—THOMAS MONSON

Don't write so that you can be understood,
write so that you can't be misunderstood.

—WILLIAM TAFT

The good listener is not only popular everywhere,
but after a while he gets to know something.

—WILSON MISNER

I not only use all the brains that I
have, but all that I can borrow.

—WOODROW WILSON

Be content with what you have
but not with who you are.

—ANONYMOUS

Drive like an old person and you'll
live long enough to be one.

—ANONYMOUS

Early bird gets the worm, but the
second mouse gets the cheese.

—ANONYMOUS

For every problem there is a solution, even
if it is learning to live with the problem.

—ANONYMOUS

If it sounds too good to be true, it is.

—ANONYMOUS

If you don't practice what you preach,
what you preach won't be practiced.

—ANONYMOUS

Measure twice, cut once.

—ANONYMOUS

Perseverance alone does not assure success. No amount of stalking will lead to game in a field that has none.

—ANONYMOUS

The wise learn more from fools than the fools learn from the wise.

—ANONYMOUS

Time is money, use it wisely.

—ANONYMOUS

You will always pay for a shortcut in the long run.

—ANONYMOUS

Poor is the pupil who does not surpass his master.

—LEONARDO DA VINCI

If you're the smartest one in the
room, find another room.

—JACK WELCH

The wise person learns to enjoy
things without owning them.

—ANONYMOUS

True genius resides in the capacity
for evaluation of uncertain, hazardous
and conflicting information.

—WINSTON CHURCHILL

But let your yes be yes and your no be no.

—MATTHEW 5:37

Let advance worrying become
advance thinking and planning.

—WINSTON CHURCHILL

Common sense is not so common.

—VOLTAIRE

Do not let what you cannot do
interfere with what you can.

—JOHN WOODEN

Millions saw the apple fall, but Newton
was the one who asked why.

—BERNARD BARUCH

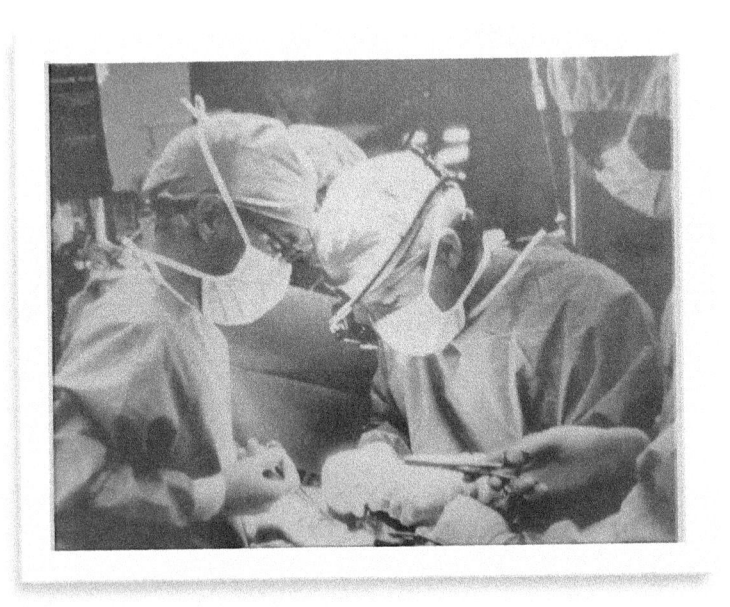

In the operating room (on the right), VA
Hospital, Oklahoma City, 1984

Work

He who rows the boat has no time to rock it.

—BILL COPELAND

Don't mistake activity for achievement.

—JOHN WOODEN

Well done is better than well said.

—BENJAMIN FRANKLIN

There is no fatigue so wearisome as that which comes from lack of work.

—CHARLES SPURGEON

A creative man is motivated by the desire to achieve, not by the desire to beat others.

—AYN RAND

There is no time for cut-and-dried monotony. There is time for work. And time for love. That leaves no other time.

—COCO CHANEL

It takes as much stress to be a success as it does to be a failure.

—EMILIO JAMES TRUJILLO

Never tell people how to do things. Tell them what you want to achieve, and they will surprise you with their ingenuity.

—GENERAL GEORGE PATTON

It takes less time to do a thing right, then it does to explain why you did it wrong.

—HENRY WADSWORTH LONGFELLOW

QUOTES & NOTES

It's what you learn after
you know it all that counts.

—JOHN WOODEN

Laziness is just getting your
rest before you're tired.

—JULES RENARD

When I rest I rust.

—LATIN PROVERB

No one ever drowned in sweat.

—LOU HOLTZ

I am always doing that which I cannot do,
in order that I may learn how to do it.

—PABLO PICASSO

The best way to make your dreams
come true is to wake up.

—PAUL VALLERY

Plan your work, work your plan.

—PHIL FLORA

Good enough isn't good enough if it can be
better, better isn't good enough if it can be best.

—RICK RIGSBY

People have been known to achieve more as a result of working with others than against them.

—ANONYMOUS

Family and friends, Cloud Gate at Millennium Park, Chicago, 2019

Who you are is more important than what you do.

—SETH BUECHLEY

Success is dependent on effort.

—SOPHOCLES

I have not failed. I've just found
10,000 ways that don't work.

—THOMAS EDISON

The only place where success comes
before work is in the dictionary.

—VIDAL SASSOON

There are no traffic jams along the extra mile.

—ROGER STAUBACH

Success is the ability to go from one failure
to another with no loss of enthusiasm.

—WINSTON CHURCHILL

No matter how you feel, get up,
dress up and show up.

—ANONYMOUS

The world is run by people who make lists.

—ANONYMOUS

Think like an owner, not an employee.

—ANONYMOUS

**Nothing is really work
unless you would rather
be doing something else.**

—SIR JAMES M. BARRIE

Aubrey at the beach, 1996

Kenya, Africa, 2018

Every morning in Africa, a gazelle wakes up. It knows it must run faster than the fastest lion or it will be killed. Every morning in Africa, a lion wakes up. It knows it must outrun the slowest gazelle or it will starve to death. It doesn't matter whether you are a lion or a gazelle. When the sun comes up, you'd better be running.

—ANONYMOUS

Whatever you are, be a good one.

—WILLIAM THACKERAY

If you have read this book from start to finish, then these last pages are a farewell of sorts. Here are two of my favorite blessings I shared with my children as they departed for college to make a life of their own.

QUOTES & NOTES

I WISH YOU ENOUGH. . .

I wish you enough sun to keep your attitude bright no matter how gray the day may appear.

I wish you enough rain to appreciate the sun even more.

I wish you enough happiness to keep your spirit alive and everlasting.

I wish you enough pain so that even the smallest of joys in life may appear bigger.

I wish you enough gain to satisfy your wanting.

I wish you enough loss to appreciate all that you possess.

I wish you enough hellos to get you through the final good-bye.

IRISH BLESSING

May the road rise up to meet you. May the wind be always at your back. May the sun shine warm upon your face; the rains fall soft upon your fields and until we meet again, may God hold you in the palm of His hand.

ACKNOWLEDGMENTS

First, I would like to thank my wife Michelle for her constant support, both during my surgical career and my rather circuitous journey after retirement from practice. No sacrifice of hers ever seems too much to support her family and friends.

Second, thanks to Aubrey, Alex and Mary, who have survived and indeed flourished despite amateur parenting. They have continually prioritized family over what seemingly may have been more attractive alternatives, and their love for each other is a source of recurring gratitude for their parents.

Finally, many thanks to Becky Bayne, who carried this novice author and his fledgling manuscript across the finish line with an admirable blend of advice, experience, and encouragement.

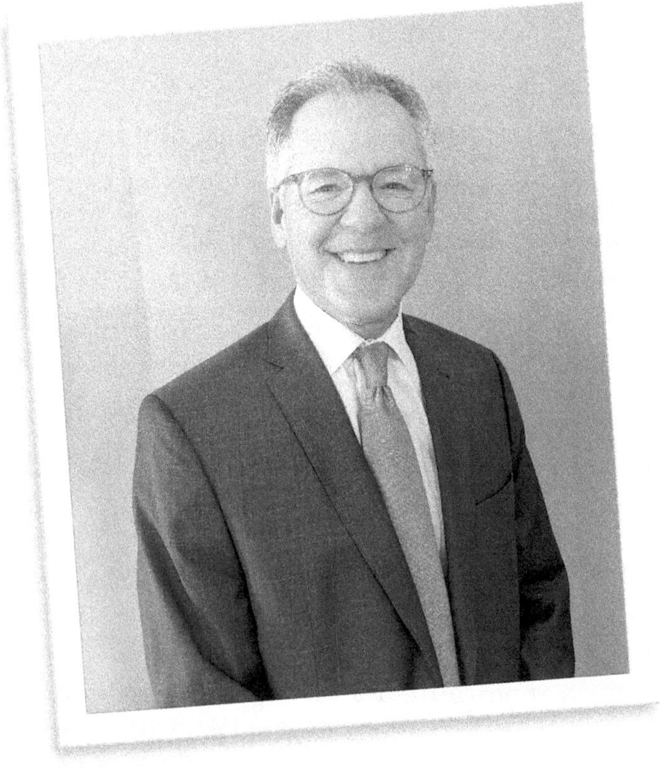

ABOUT THE AUTHOR

John Austin is a former cardiovascular surgeon, married with three grown children. After retirement from cardiac surgery in 2010, he has been involved in healthcare IT, numerous overseas medical missions, and several healthcare startups. He has also been employed as a team doctor for the Tennessee Titans, spent 3 years as a fee-based provider for the U.S. Department of Defense, and currently is a telemedicine physician. John is very active in his church and is an avid amateur golfer.

QUOTES & NOTES

A Dad's Best Advice for His Kids

JOHN AUSTIN

LEAVE A REVIEW!

For independently published authors like myself, reviews mean the world! Please consider rating and reviewing this book on the platform from which it was purchased.